POETIC VOYAGES ROCHDALE

Edited by Dave Thomas

First published in Great Britain in 2001 by
YOUNG WRITERS
Remus House,
Coltsfoot Drive,
Peterborough, PE2 9JX
Telephone (01733) 890066

HB ISBN 0 75433 104 0
SB ISBN 0 75433 105 9

FOREWORD

Young Writers was established in 1991 with the aim to promote creative writing in children, to make reading and writing poetry fun.

This year once again, proved to be a tremendous success with over 88,000 entries received nationwide.

The Poetic Voyages competition has shown us the high standard of work and effort that children are capable of today. It is a reflection of the teaching skills in schools, the enthusiasm and creativity they have injected into their pupils shines clearly within this anthology.

The task of selecting poems was therefore a difficult one but nevertheless, an enjoyable experience. We hope you are as pleased with the final selection in *Poetic Voyages Rochdale* as we are.

CONTENTS

Heybrook CP School

St Patrick's Primary School

The Poems

SPIDER, SPIDER

Spider, spider
You'll never catch a hawk inside that web

It's made for flies and not for hawks
Is what the spider said

Spider, spider
Why is the law so like a spider's web?

It catches the flies but not the hawks
Is what the spider said

Zaide Elizabeth Nicholas (11)
Bullough Moor County Primary School

CHOCOLATE FRIGHT

I went to get some hot chocolate.
I saw a frightening ghost.
It had a rattling chain
And a big moustache.
It was very frightening
When it laughed
In the dark.

Stephanie Cullen (11)
Bullough Moor County Primary School

THE FAT CAT

There was a man who had a cat,
He fed it so well it grew fat.
It grew and grew more fat and fat,
Too big for its basket, it slept on its mat.
And then one day
In its pot
It ate its food
And then it popped!

Anthony Nuttall (11)
Bullough Moor County Primary School

FLYING, FURRY LITTLE CHAP

He's a furry, flying little chap
From 65 million years back,
He has a beak and two feet,
He flies around searching for meat,
Don't meet him at night
You'll wake up and have a fright,
As this little charm,
Bites off your arm.
He has sharp teeth
And a very long beak,
He might just chop off
Your hands and feet.

Rebecca Williams (10)
Bullough Moor County Primary School

THE GHOST

I was walking down the street,
When I saw a ghost.
I was scared to the bone,
She gave a loud moan.
I ran away fast,
And jumped in car
And left with a blast.

Nigel Phipps (11)
Bullough Moor County Primary School

CHILL OUT!

'Chill out!' said Mum, 'And start having fun!'
'How can I have fun if I have an empty tum?'
'OK, OK, chill out,' said Mum, 'don't worry,
I'll get you a big, fat plum.'
'Mmmm,' said Becky, halfway through her food,
'Finally,' said Mum, 'you're in a happy mood!'

Terri-Lee Reeve (11)
Bullough Moor County Primary School

THE ZOO

I went to the zoo
To see a bear
He was very vicious
He picked me up through the bars
And ate me ~ how delicious!

If he ate me,
How could I write
This lovely poem today?
Because I'm stuck between his teeth
And causing tooth decay!

Michelle Hart (10)
Bullough Moor County Primary School

THE GORGOSAURUS

Thump! Thump! Thump!
The Gorgosaurus knocks down a tree stump!
It stands up high
It has two angry eyes
It has a round chubby body
Its got big ears like Noddy
Its got some sharp claws
On those huge strong paws
Its teeth are sharper than razors
Its skin is as red as a Siddal Moor blazer
Thump! Thump! Thump!
The Gorgosaurus knocks down a tree stump!

Daniel Greenhalgh (10)
Bullough Moor County Primary School

LITTLE RED RAP

Just on the edge
Of a deep, dark wood
Lived a girl called
Little Red riding Hood
Her grandmother lived
Not far away
So Red went to pay her
A visit one day
And the big bad wolf
Who knew her plan
He turned his nose
And ran and ran
He ran till he came
To her grandmother's door
Then he locked her up
With a great big roar
He took her place
In her nice warm bed
And he waited there
For little Miss Red

Michael Lee (11)
Bullough Moor County Primary School

THE UNKNOWN

Do aliens really exist?
Are they out there in the mist?
Will we find them light years later?
We've already seen their huge crater.

Some of greed look for riches,
Some strange hunt for witches.
Those with all black magic,
Deadly curses all so tragic
Hidden in a haunted house,
What! Was that a mouse?
Creaky floorboards? Is it mice?
Could it be? It's a poltergeist!

A spook and a spell, it's all very well.
A ghost with the most?

We can look, we can stare,
But what really can be there?
From the germ we have grown
None will find the unknown.

Jack Robertson (10)
Bullough Moor County Primary School

MY CAT

My cat is cute
My cat is dumb
My cat is really, really fun
He'll bring in birds
Won't say any words
He's mad as a hatter
Gets fatter and fatter
He's lovely and cuddly
And never gets muddy
And never gets mad at you.

Katie Ryan (10)
Bullough Moor County Primary School

AUTUMN MAGIC

Notice how the leaves
Turn orange, red and brown
Conker fights are everywhere
In probably every town

Tiny little helicopters
Twirling from the trees
Squirrels eat the acorns
Off the tall oak trees.

Zoe Reynolds (11)
Bullough Moor County Primary School

ON THE BEACH

At the beach there's lots of fish
Swimming around in a big blue dish
In the ocean that's rough
There's boats, plenty enough.
On the sand there's crabs
Even a worm
That's one sight that made me squirm.
There's children playing having fun
Whilst in the sky there's a blazing sun.
Palm trees are still just like a broken mill
There's no summer's breeze to move all the trees
The wind picks up and blows off a hat
As well as the sand where I'm sat
I saw an ice cream van so I bought a double-decker
Then a seagull came and pinched it with its pecker
The sight of the seagull gave me such a fright
So I went to the apartment and stayed there all night
Today was such a busy day
So I retired to my bed
And went to sleep straight away.

Rebecca Goulden (11)
Bullough Moor County Primary School

THE GHOST

I was watching TV
And eating popcorn
Until the doorbell went ding dong
I got up to get it
But no-one was there
But a toy grizzly bear!
I shut the door
And ran upstairs
Into my bedroom and it was there
I screamed and screamed
And screamed some more
Then I fainted on the floor.

Sophie Taylor-Noble (11)
Bullough Moor County Primary School

TEAMWORK

Two leopards wearing
    A terrible frown.
They wriggled and jiggled
    And jumped up and down.

They twisted, insisted,
    'I can count my spots.'
Then tumbled and grumbled,
    'I'm tied up in knots!'

They scowled and they growled,
    They hadn't a clue.
Then, all of a sudden,
    They knew what to do.

They bounced and announced,
    As they shook their great paws,
'You can count my spots . . .
    And I will count yours!'

Emma Kay (10)
Bullough Moor County Primary School

AUTUMN

Autumn time when the grass is green
The yellow sun shining in the sky
The clouds so grey they are worn out and battered
Autumn time is a happy time

Kimberley Walker (10)
Bullough Moor County Primary School

GAME BOY

Game Boy games are red, yellow and blue.
All in colour, all shiny and new.
Not like the old ones that are poo!
I love my Game Boy colour
And so would you!

Ryan Hayes (11)
Bullough Moor County Primary School

THE CIDER MAN

There was an old farmer in Devon,
Who woke up at half past eleven,
He drank lots of cider
And ate a fat spider
And ended up sleeping in Heaven.

Ashleigh Whittaker (11)
Bullough Moor County Primary School

STRANDED ON AN ISLAND

Stranded on an island
With nowhere else to go
Nobody to talk to
Nobody I know
It may have all the money
And riches you can buy
But money can't buy happiness
On that you can rely.

April Louise Marland (10)
Bullough Moor County Primary School

TEN WHITE SNOWMEN

Ten white snowmen having a lovely time
One got hay fever, then there were nine.
Nine white snowmen losing weight
One got too skinny, and then there were eight.
Eight white snowmen going to Devon
One got sunburnt, then there were seven.
Seven white snowmen eating Weetabix
One ate too much, then there were six.
Six white snowmen looking at a hive
A bee stung one, then there were five.
Five white snowmen messing with the door
One got his head stuck, then there were four.
Four white snowmen watching TV
One got square eyes, then there were three.
Three white snowmen with the flu
One got pneumonia, then there were two.
Two white snowmen with a light that shone
They burst into flames, then there were *none*.

James Noonan (9)
Bullough Moor County Primary School

TEN WHITE SNOWMEN

Ten white snowmen drinking wine
One got drunk, then there were nine.
Nine white snowmen all overweight
One went on a diet, then there were eight.
Eight white snowmen going to Devon
One got sunburnt, and then there were seven.
Seven white snowmen eating Weetabix
One ate too much, then there were six.
Six white snowmen standing on the drive
One fell on the road, then there were five.
Five white snowmen all feeling sore
One went to hospital, then there were four.
Four white snowmen watching TV
One got square eyes, then there were three.
Three white snowmen all got the flu
One got pneumonia, then there were two.
Two white snowmen having fun
One was miserable, then there was one.
One white snowman feeling all alone
Then it vanished, and then there was none.

Sophie Maxwell (9)
Bullough Moor County Primary School

THE SEASONS

Leaves fall in autumn,
Flowers grow in spring.
In winter there is lots of snow,
In summer - everything.

Sometimes spring brings sunshine,
Sometimes it brings rain.
This weather is good for farmers,
Growing wheat and grain.

We're off to the beach in summer,
Back home again in July.
Then we'll have to wait again,
Till winter passes by.

The trees are bare in autumn,
Their leaves are on the ground.
They're red, green, brown and gold,
And make a crunching sound.

In winter there is snow and ice,
It's not exactly hot.
In December it is Christmas,
With hot soup in a pot.

I hope you've enjoyed this 20-line ode,
About the seasons of the year.
I hope you've find it very nice,
And very pleasant to hear.

Edward Sargent (10)
Healey Primary School

ANIMALS

You know that old insect the cricket
They'll find a small apple and kick it
They'll slice it in half
And then make you barf
And that's just the typical cricket

You know that small 'un the frog
Who'll always bath in a bog
He'll sit like a spy
Then eat a big fly
And they get chased by the dogs

You know that slime ball the fish
Which humans eat in a dish
Some jump like birds
And swim in some herds
That's what so dumb about fish

And we come to human beings
Which have the very most feelings
They'll eat a bit of this
Then have a kiss
And that's the smart Alec, the human.

Wesley Hilton-Gani (10)
Healey Primary School

PIRATE SHIP

I once saw a pirate ship,
With a skull and crossbones flag,
On the flag there was a rip,
It looked like a right old rag.

The pirate ship stopped,
At the end of the sea,
My heart nearly popped,
The pirates stared at me.

They pulled me aboard the ship,
'What are you doing here?'
I was taking a dip,'
I replied with fear.

I had to get out of there,
I knew it,
They were like a pack of grizzly bears,
They would throw me in a pit.

I jumped overboard,
I swam for about a mile,
'He's getting away,' they roared
I trod more water than there is in the River Nile.

I swam to the shore,
Dripping wet,
That was far from a bore,
Now I don't need to fret.

I saw the ship again
Oh no! What a pain
Their heads went low
That was the last time I saw them
Thank God!

Heather Bibbington (10)
Healey Primary School

THE FLYING PIG

Once, long ago,
As my grandpa said so,
Something up in the sky,
A pig that could fly.

Now we know not
'Cos we must have forgot,
How he learned to do it,
'Cept his guy said he knew it.

Although no one listens to that geezer
He's got as much brains as the Tower of Pisa
I've seen a needle that winked its eye
But never a pig that can fly!

He whirled and spun and looped-the-loop
And a new thing he called 'the scoop'
Now, one day he hitched a ride
On an aeroplane that did glide

Inside the plane was a VIP
Halfway through a sentence he
Spotted the pig flying around
'If you catch that, I'll give you one pound!'

At this dreadful deal
Piggy did a big squeal
He flew and he hid
Behind a kid

Seven years later
'Twas spotted by a 'gator
And swallowed whole
Down Snappy's pie hole.

Peter William Hodkinson (11)
Healey Primary School

UFOs

UFOs way up high,
UFOs in the sky,
Flying about, spooking us out,
Everyone shouting, without a doubt.

UFOs way up high,
UFOs in the sky,
Laser rays shooting high and low,
Ouch, they got my toe!

UFOs way up high,
UFOs in the sky,
Go away, go away, I say,
No! We're here to stay.

UFOs way up high,
UFOs in the sky,
Nobody knows where they're from,
Maybe they're from the planet Zon.

Lauren Jade Walsh (10)
Healey Primary School

FISH

Every time you see a fish
You must make a little wish
They're sometimes gold
Some like it cold

Plecks are black
They have a curved back
Their food is flaky
Their tails are shaky

When they win races
They have happy faces
They have two big fins
And wet silky skins.

Hannah Wood (10)
Healey Primary School

DREAMLAND

Take a journey to Dreamland,
Where nothing is as it seems.
Yellow trees and purple sand,
Really makes you beam!

Light pink clouds and dark green sky,
Which rains a few cats and dogs!
And the first thing that meets the eye,
A bright red, swirly fog!

Bright blue cows and flying pigs,
Are way above the ordinary!
And gracefully floating in the sky,
You'll spot the Virgin Mary!

Surprisingly, waiting to meet you,
You'll find your very best mate,
In your cossie (which is brand new)
You can go bathing in chocolate!

Then you hear your alarm clock,
Which ends your happiness,
There is a ship waiting at the dock,
You're in your room (it's a mess)!

Georgia Sunderland (10)
Healey Primary School

MY CLASS

Natalie, Peter, Jamie and Oliver are tall,
Rachel, Scott R, Nikul and Wesley are small,
Paul, Heidi and Robert play football,
Hannah, Jack, Matthew and Becca T have the same colour hair,
Lauren and Edward are a right strange pair,
Heather, Georgia and I like to talk,
Mrs Whitworth uses her chalk,
Kirsty and Nickolas are the best of friends,
Joshua J, Richard S and Gareth play pretends,
Joshua R, Ross and James seem to enjoy games,
Oh deary me! Guess who I forgot?
It's Richard N, Joshua T and the other Scott!

Rebecca Louise Parry (11)
Healey Primary School

THE RIVER

The river's steadily flowing faster and faster,
Until it smashes down the mountain.
Cracking all the rocks carrying them away,
The river's flowing on its journey.

The river's flowing calm and smooth,
Through the spooky black gigantic forest.
Slowly it started to gleam in the sun,
The river's flowing on its journey.

The river starts to grow larger,
Gleaming brightly in the sunlight.
Slowly it enters the sea,
The river's journey is finally over.

James Collier (10)
Healey Primary School

LIZARDS

I like lizards because
Some are black
And some are white
Most are green.
Some are big
Geckos can climb up walls
Most are small
But the ones I like the most are
Chameleons
Which are good
At camouflaging.

Richard Shepherd (10)
Healey Primary School

PLAYTIME MAYHEM

In the playground it is noisy and loud.
All the children scattering around.
Oh no, here comes a huge big cloud.
Don't forget the girls playing, making lots more sound.
Playtime mayhem is back again.

When the teachers are on duty.
They think they have lots of beauty (yeah right)
The year six trying to rule
They wish they could play lots of pool.

When the boys are playing football.
And the girls are going to the ball.
At home time mums and dads come to school
I think school is rather cool.

Jack Glasgow (11)
Healey Primary School

THE COMET

The comet, the comet shooting away,
Comet, comet, come to play,
When it's done, shoot to the sun
And then come back another day.

Shoot to Saturn
Come back and give us some platinum.

Now your voyage is done
Here's what you have won
A kick up the bum.

Gareth Dearden (11)
Healey Primary School

POISONING

'Mum, I think there's something wrong in what I ate,
There is some green stuff on my plate.
It is my last day until my fate,
I've got food poisoning, I'm gonna ring my mate!'

Dear my precious, precious diary,
It's my last day on Earth, it's rather scary.
After today I'll join Great Grandma Mary,
Goodbye, dear brother, in the military.

I said my prayers, but I found I just had wind,
It could be worse, and at least I've not sinned.

Robert Shepherd (10)
Healey Primary School

CATS AND DOGS ALWAYS FIGHT

Cats and dogs always fight
They miaow and bark through the night
There's a bang and a crash and something will smash
I think I might just explode

If I had one wish
I would turn them to fish
And put them in separate bowls

I wish I could
Just lose them for good
And never see them again.

Ross Hopwood (10)
Healey Primary School

My Tiger, Rob

My tiger, Rob
eats a lot of corn on the cob
but he's quite a nelly
since he tries to eat his belly
and if you smelt his rear end
you, my friend,
would run a hundred miles.

Joshua Jackson (10)
Healey Primary School

WARTIME

Bombs are dropping, bombs are dropping
Whilst the farmers are doing some cropping.
Hitler's bad
Drawing strategies on an A4 pad.
Evacuation on the train
While the soldiers are in some pain.

The Spitfires are flying above
When the children are making a move.
Now you see the smouldering holes
You can look at the running voles.
Germany versus Britain.

Jamie Anderson (11)
Healey Primary School

MY FIRST DAY AT MY NEW SCHOOL

I stood outside my classroom,
feeling shy and looking red.
I felt my doom and gloom,
and wished I'd stayed in bed.

I looked at all the people,
who were glancing back at me.
I looked up at a steeple,
oh please look down at me.

The teacher came towards me,
and asked if I would sit down.
I fell over my chair,
and felt like a clown.

I got up very slowly,
and walked over to my desk.
I felt very lonely,
and also a big pest.

The day was getting worse and worse,
I'm sure someone put on a curse.
At last the school bell rang,
oops another big clang!

Abby Jayne Hickingbotham (9)
Healey Primary School

BATH TIME TROUBLE

I was sat in the bath,
having a laugh,
when I got myself into trouble,
as I was suddenly attacked by a bubble.

The bubble was big,
it hit my mum's wig,
she got in a fit,
I nearly lost my kit!

I got a red bum,
as red as a plum,
I drove her round the bend,
I'm sorry, that's the end.

Kathryn Rebecca Preston (9)
Healey Primary School

I'M A MONSTER

I could not sleep one night
I was turning
Twisting, I could not sleep
My belly's churning.

I am going Hairy
I'm going green
I'm getting razor teeth
I'm starting to lean.

My hair's spiky and red
My nails are gold
My hands are turning blue
And my face is old.

My feet are yellow *wow!*
My toes are bent
My eyes are really dark
My ears became vents.

I looked in the mirror
I'm a . . . *monster!*
Help, somebody, help me
I ran to Munster.

When I got to Munster
There were lots of
Ugly monsters like me
With ugly pet moths.

The other monsters took
Me to a hill
To look over the sea
They gave me a pill

Suddenly I woke up
It was a dream.

Samantha Taylor (9)
Healey Primary School

THE LITTLE CHEEKY DEVIL

One day at school,
In the swimming pool,
I looked up to the sky,
I saw a very ugly thing,
Which made a few babies cry.

My mother saw that beastly thing,
Not so long ago,
But when she saw it this time,
She screamed, 'Oh no, oh no, oh no!'

The reason that she did that,
Was because she was mad,
That little cheeky devil thing,
Ate her little cat.

I don't know why it followed me,
It must be needing a home,
I asked my mum and 'No' she said,
'Just take it down below.'

I went and asked my dad,
And he said just the same,
That little cheeky devil thing,
It doesn't look very tame.

Helen Youngblut (9)
Healey Primary School

THE ROBBER

There was a lady from Peru
Who might sing along with you.
She had a pet, whose name was King
She had a suspicious thing.

I found out she's a mean robber
On her cheek there was slobber.
There was the most precious diamond
That she burgled from Primeland.

The police had to stop her
All dressed in her white fur.
They caught the mean lady
'Cos she was so shady.

The lady was put in jail
Well, that was in the gale.
She lost the most precious diamond
And it was returned to Primeland.

Jake Harris (9)
Healey Primary School

MY CAT, NELLY

I once had a cat called Nelly,
Who had a sore belly,
Plus he slept in a welly,
So we took him to the vet,
He said, 'Oh what a lovely pet,
He will be back by tomorrow
But he will have wind though.'
'Oh no!'

Natalie Farrar (11)
Healey Primary School

My Worst Friend

I have a worst friend,
He sends me round the bend,
I hate him so much,
I felt like hitting him at lunch.

He picks his big nose,
Licks his big smelly toes,
Nobody likes him,
Except a pretty girl called Kim.

He has got blond hair,
He likes to eat fat pears,
He loves all the girls,
Who have dark brown hair with big curls.

Ra'ana Javed (9)
Healey Primary School

THE WITCH FROM WATERLOO

This strange old witch from Waterloo,
Came home one day and said;
'Goodness gracious, what thing are you?'
'You must have lost your head.'

Suddenly the witch jumped right back,
'How dare you be so rude;
Any more and you'll get the sack.'
'You're fat and in the nude.'

'I'm off upstairs to get my clothes,
So see you in a tic;
I need some more of those small loavies,
Don't dare mess with that pic.'

The witch never came down the stairs,
The boy shouted, 'Woa Hoo!'
Me on my own had not any cares,
The witch from Waterloo.

Thomas Andrew Sutcliffe (9)
Healey Primary School

THE WITCHES' CAVE

A girl was trotting home from school
She spun around and saw a ghoul
The ghoul, he grabbed her round the neck
The girl, she screamed, 'Oh heck!'

The ghoul dragged the girl to a cave
She started to cry, 'Come and save.'
Tears were streaming down her face
The ghoul replied, 'Watch this space.'

The cave doors slowly creaked open
She closed her eyes hopin' and hopin'
Inside there were three witches
They had a face full of stitches

They snatched the girl from the white ghoul
They chucked the girl into a pool
The pool was made out of green slime
She wasn't saved in time

   I'm sorry, that's the end.

Shauni Dalton (10)
Healey Primary School

THE ELEGY OF MR COX

There once was a ferocious ox
Whose evil name was Mr Cox,
He woke one dark night
Preparing to fight

Upon the heath to meet Macbeth,
He then started to lose his breath
He fought so hard back,
His sword started to crack
Which certainly meant his death.

Jack Lyons (10)
Healey Primary School

MY FUNNY DREAM

One night I had a funny dream
As I was laid in bed
It really made me shout and scream
It really hurt my head

My dad came rushing to my room
He asked if I were scared
I said I'd heard a big loud boom
Get ready, be prepared

He went out of my room again
After he'd tucked me in
I bet he thought I was insane
He'd put me in the bin

I tried and tried to get to sleep
But I'd already tried
I just kept having little peeps
I knew I would get fried

Eventually I said night night
Because I had to go
Please somebody turn out the light
Oh no! Oh no! Oh no!

Courtney Trainor (9)
Healey Primary School

CHANGED INTO AN ALIEN

This is a good story
Listen closely and hear me say . . .
If you scare easily,
You'd better choose another way . . .

This good story began
When I started to feel strange . . .
My voice went all squeaky,
Suddenly I started to change . . .

My hands went all purple
My body went a pinky shade . . .
My feet went big and fat,
It wouldn't stop until I paid . . .

I didn't want to change
I was happy the way I was . . .
I was a nice, kind girl,
I didn't want to be like boz . . .

Finally I changed back
What a bad nightmare it has been
I want to close my eyes
I wish I'd never, ever seen.

Chloe Press (10)
Healey Primary School

ZAP, THE ALIEN

There was an alien called Zap,
Who was a very tall, nice chap.
He came from the planet San-sot.
It was the shape of a plant pot.

Zap was a teacher in school,
Everyone thought he's a fool.
Just because his skin was purple,
Because he acts like a turtle.

Every night he would stay awake,
And felt like he's in a lake.
Just because they treat him bad,
Not any girls but every lad.

Something had to be done 'bout this.
Then he started to think and hiss.
I know! I think I'll leave this town,
Out here they think that I'm a clown.

So that's the end of the poem,
Now I've got to get on goin'.
No wonder that you're very sad,
Because those children were so bad.

Imogen Victoria Greenwood (10)
Healey Primary School

THE THING

I stumbled upon something brown
While I was in the park
It was wearing a big gold crown
Shaped like a whistling lark.

I wondered what this thing could be
I turned and walked away
Oh no the time, it's time for tea
What will my mother say?

My time was running out quickly
I started running fast
I felt as itchy as could be
Under my plaster cast.

I went to see the squiggly thing
After I'd had my tea
I felt a little tiny ping
Something was after me.

I looked down to the floor and then
I saw to my disgust
A really little chubby hen
It's face looked like a crust.

Emily Greensmith (10)
Healey Primary School

THE THING

One night was sleeping in bed
(I was dreaming of school)
When something hit me on the head
It looked like a big ghoul

I woke up in wonder and fright
I wanted my mummy
I held my teddy very tight
Funny feelings in the tummy

I went to switch on the big light
I was feeling quite scared
I felt something trying to bite
My cloak was getting teared

What was hiding beside my side?
I turned around to peek
The door was open very wide
All I could hear was the sink leak.

Rhian Louise Warren (9)
Healey Primary School

THE ANT MOVES OUT

An ant stood near the hill,
It was standing very still,
Until the wind blew and blew,
And the leaves went and flew.
The ant stood there feeling cold,
But until he was told,
He figured out he would move,
And then he would start to groove.
The ant thought and figured out,
He would move without a doubt,
And make his own ant-hill,
Near the old rusty mill.
And there he went the next day,
And found some cloth and some hay,
And so he built his own ant-hill,
Next to the rusty mill.

Joseph James Oliver (10)
Healey Primary School

THE SWIMMING GALA

There was a fish called Larna,
Who was in a swimming gala.
All the people are in white,
They are ready and bright.
They were all sat in the chairs.

The refs have got their guns,
Now their eating buns.
They say, 'Take your marks, go.'
They were very slow.
Splash, splash, splash they go.

Amy Louise Blackburn (10)
Healey Primary School

A DRAGON

A dragon has a snout
Where fire comes out.
It has some spikes
That can scratch metal.
It has a tail
With a spike at the end.
A dragon has some wings
That could carry me 5000 metres high.

Josh Simpson (7)
Healey Primary School

WEATHER

Wind is the whistle.
Rain is some maracas.

Hail is the tambourine
Banging on your doorstep.
The sun is bright
And shines in your eyes.
When it shines on your window
That is brighter than that.

Sleet makes you scared
Or sometimes makes you happy.
The sun and the clouds come out until . . .
The rain came down
Oh no! Splat!

Grace Dearden (7)
Healey Primary School

MY DOG

My dog is a girl,
She gets in the way.
She barks a lot.
She is a good girl.
When I say 'sit' she does it.
That's why she's good.

Sarah Jackson (7)
Healey Primary School

WIND

The wind is strong
It pulls off my clothes
It ruins my hair
But still it blows and blows.

The wind makes the trees go swish
And the sea get rough and make a *splash.*

The wind can blow down houses
And can even smash cars.
The wind is useful for flying kites.

Leanne Grindrod (7)
Healey Primary School

FAIRIES

Fairies are sweet,
They're beautiful and neat.
They fly up and down above the street,
They twinkle and shine all night long,
Moving their wings, they sing a song.
Fairies are nice, they're like little mice,
Their wishes are better,
And every night I send them a letter.

Jessica O'Connor (8)
Healey Primary School

GOLDILOCKS

Goldilocks said
'What have we there?
A bowl of porridge,
But hot and bare.'

Goldilocks said
'This one's sweet,
But quite cold,
Not like meat.'

Goldilocks said
'This one's fine,
Yummy and scrummy,
Just like pine.'

Goldilocks said
'This chair's tall,
Hard as rock,
I'm too small.'

Goldilocks said
'This one's comfy
But too cold,
I'm too chuffy.'

Goldilocks said
'This one's bash
The best of all
Small an' *'crash.'*

Goldilocks said
(After two beds)
'I'll now go to sleep.'
And that's all she said.

Lucy Hodkinson (9)
Healey Primary School

HOMEWORK

Homework!
Every day
Homework!
Get no pay
Homework!
Hate it
Homework!
Don't rate it
Homework!
Pile on more
Homework!
What's it for?
Homework!
Mum shouting
Homework!
Me pouting
Homework!
Boring
Homework!
I'll soon be snoring
Homework!
Done . . .
Now for some fun.

Jennifer Smith (8)
Healey Primary School

BAD WEEK

Day One Monday
Bad day at school
Got shouted at 'cause I forgot my homework.

Day Two Tuesday
Now it's worse
I forgot my homework and I got sent to Mrs Talor!

Day Three Wednesday
Now it's really worse
I forgot my homework
And I got sent to Mrs Talor plus I forgot my games kit.

Day Four Thursday
Now it's really worse
I forgot my homework and got sent to Mrs Ealer,
Plus I forgot my games kit and fell asleep in lessons!

Day Five Friday
It's better, it's the last day.

Dominic Press (8)
Healey Primary School

MY DREAM

I had a dream
The best dream in the world
I liked the dream I had that night
About a butterfly flapping in the light
The butterfly flew through my hedge
Then sat on my window ledge
I had a dream
The best dream in the world.

Nadia Ul-Haq (9)
Healey Primary School

THE ROYALS

I wonder if the Queen
Is nice or very mean
Is she really quite posh?
Does she have a lot of dosh?

I wonder if the King
Does have a diamond ring
Does he have a lot of jewels
And made his courtiers look like fools?

I wonder if the Royals
Have spots, freckles or boils
It seems a small wonder
Can't turn into a worry
So I'll send them some fan-mail
To answer in a hurry!

Sarah C Young (9)
Healey Primary School

ME

I don't like to be bad,
And I don't like to be sad.
I like to be nice,
And I like rice.
I like it in the shower,
But I don't like power.
I like the stars,
Where they are.
I don't like the sun
When it shoots like a gun.

Scott Hey (7)
Healey Primary School

PETTI HETTI

There once was a girl called Hetti,
Who was a little bit petti,
She went to a wedding and threw confetti,
And that's the story of Hetti.

Kirsty Brewer (10)
Healey Primary School

FOOTBALL DAY

Children running
Children getting hurt
Ball shooting
Children scoring
Whistle blowing
Children cheering
Goalie jumping
Goalie missing!

Timothy Palmer (8)
Healey Primary School

MY ROOM

My room, my room
Dirty, dirty, dirty room
Makes lots and lots of heads boom
My dirty room

My room, my room
Cool, cool, cool room
Lots of posters that boom
My cool room

My room, my room
Clean, clean, clean room
Looks like a polish bomb went boom
My clean room.

Peter Holland (8)
Healey Primary School

KINGS AND QUEENS

There was a King Henry
Who had a wife Wendy
She is poetic and friendly
But very bendy

There was a Queen who didn't tackle
Her husband liked a battle
He had a good built fort
But lost the battle.

Nathan Antony Hardman (9)
Healey Primary School

UP ABOVE THE DARK BLUE SKY

Up above the dark blue sky
Where the stars go tumbling by
Where the first men lived on the moon
Do you think they saw a big baboon
And a giant red caterpillar
Whooshing down the water flume?

Do you think they played with big red balls?
I think they eat fish and veggieburgers
And watched the stars and lay on the moon
To watch the sun go down.
I think they swam through the sky
As the children settled down.

Paige Hilton-Gani (9)
Healey Primary School

THE WHETHER WORM

I don't know whether I will go to bed
but the whether worm does.
Look, is it a bird? Is it a plane?
It looks like a flying worm to me.
It's the whether worm.
He knows what the whether is going to be.
Oh yes he does.

Wesley Adam Jefferies (8)
Healey Primary School

THE GOOD OLD HOCKEY GAME

Playing hockey
Opposition cocky
Hit puck
Good luck
Scream, shout
Everyone's out.

Thomas Hammond (8)
Healey Primary School

FOOTBALL

Football is great, that is my favourite sport
Oh no! He's missed a penalty.
Oh noo! Here comes Trouble, the dog.
Trouble comes and scores.
Bad dog, Trouble.
And all the United fans go 'Boo' for Trouble.
Law in football is not to foul.
Law is not to be nasty to the referee.

James O'Neill (8)
Healey Primary School

ME AND MY BEST FRIEND

Me and my best friend play together.
Me and my best friend stay together.
I like cross country, she likes maths.
She always helps me with I'm stuck,
And sometimes brings me luck.
We like to dance, we like to sing,
We like to do the same things.
Me and my best friend are always together.
I hope we stay best friends forever and ever.
    I like my best friend.

Holly Bradbury (7)
Healey Primary School

SPOOKY

S ilent, it is dark and spooky.

P eek down the dark, damp, muddy, spooky twitch.

O h-no, there's a vampire.

O uch! It has got large fangs to bite me with.

K eep out of sight.

Y ikes, I'm scared.

Charley Slade (7)
Healey Primary School

Snow

In the winter when it snows
The wind blows, blows, blows.
Sometimes when the sun comes out
Everybody shouts, shouts, shouts.
When their snowmen melt away
Children say come another day.
Everybody wears warm clothes
And everybody loves it when it *snows!*

Imogen D'Roza (8)
Healey Primary School

SNOW

When I go out and it snows.
   Everything blows.

I make a snowman.
And if I make a good one.
He lasts like a lamb.

If he gets too hot.
   He goes like a knot.

Samantha Gregory (8)
Healey Primary School

FURRY FRIENDS

My friend, birdy, always pecks
And my giraffe has a long neck
Giggles, the monkey is very cheeky
Look! There he is.
The mouse is very sneaky and creepy.
Nelly, the elephant, is large, large, large.
Gypsy Pipsy is a dog ~ he's busy in the yard.
The cat is friendly, she never scratches.
My teddy has got patches all over him.
Oinks is the smelliest of all.
The horse calls at night.
These are my friends,
They never bite you
So don't be scared of them.

Laura Archibald (8)
Healey Primary School

SPACE

S   pacecraft flying,
P   lanets everywhere.
A   liens on bright stars,
C   old spooky space.
E   xcellent is space.

Olivia Sunderland (8)
Healey Primary School

SPACE

In space there are over 200 stars.
Jupiter is the furthest away from earth.

Halley's comet is probably the most powerful
The sun is the hottest thing.

The Milky Way galaxy has little holes in it.
It controls the stars. It makes them move about.

The Asteroid Belt is three stars. It has this kind of line.
It joins on to each other.

Voyager is kind of a planet with little holes.
You would not be able to find it.

Christopher Brierley (8)
Healey Primary School

PLAYSTATION

I love to play on my PlayStation
The discs are shiny and bright
I play on it in the evening
If my mother says it's all right.

I love to play Crash, Tombi and Smack Down too.
I have lots of games, full of action.
Would you like to come and play too?

Ben Westerman (8)
Healey Primary School

FIREWORKS

Fireworks are exciting.
When we go to the park and get sparklers
Their colours sparkle in the dark.
Some are called dragons and fountains.
Their colours are red, orange, blue and green.
They are quite noisy.
And could scare animals.
Up, up they go, colourful and bright in the dark night.
They are shiny.
Bangers and rockets are really loud.

Bang!

Sabreena Hayee (7)
Healey Primary School

OW THUNDER!

It's nearly dark,
Light will come on as the timer ticks,
Birds weren't singing like a lark,
Thunder rumbling over my head,
Lightning strays over near a boat called Ark,
The thunder is off the house, thunder rumbled,
Crack, the light's out and it is dark,
    Ow Thunder!

Matthew Crump (10)
Healey Primary School

A MAN FROM OKET

There was a man from Oket
Who went for a ride in a rocket
The rocket went bang
His ears went twang
And he found his nose in his pocket!

Hadiyah Karim (10)
Heybrook CP School

CATS

Big cats
Small cats
Thin cats
Fat cats
Cats
Cats
Cats
Cats
Cats
They like rats
For their snacks.

Madia Ayub
Heybrook CP School

THE BEAR WITH GROOVY SHOES ON HIS EARS

The other day I met a bear
with groovy shoes on his ears.
He went to a shop to get a beer,
but the shopkeeper said
he mustn't have a beer,
when he has got groovy shoes
on his ears.

Mohammid Ali (11)
Heybrook CP School

BIRTHDAY

It's my birthday
I don't know what to do
I've got a strawberry cake
And I know that's true
With all the balloons
And lovely cakes
Especially made for me
My mum said enjoy your day
But I don't believe a thing
I never had a piece of the cake
That was especially made for me.

Zakia Ilyas (11)
Heybrook CP School

WU-TANG-CLAN

Wu-Tang-Clan
Professional singers
Top at rapping
Friends of the Westside
They only look after their group.

Marufur Rahman (11)
Heybrook CP School

BIRDS

I feel like a bird,
Singing all the time,
Flapping my feathery wings.
I feel like a bird
A bird which is just
Like me!

Halima Parveen (10)
Heybrook CP School

THE LION!

There was a lion
It had sharp teeth
The lion is a predator
It's big and fat
It will eat me
It will eat all of us
It will eat you and me!

Nazia Bi (10)
Heybrook CP School

FOOD

Strawberries are red,
juicy and delicious,
as red as a beautiful rose,

Apples are green, crunchy,
and hard,
as green as a grasshopper,

Carrots are orange,
delicious and solid,
as orange as an orange,

Cucumbers are green,
delicious and hard,
hard as a rock
I said.

Imran Mohammed (8)
Heybrook CP School

THE BIG FAT BULLY

There was once a big fat bully
His name was Sarvar Gangully
He was walking down my street with a conker
I said to him you're a plonker
He turned around and I frowned
And he grinned like a clown
I had a chill down my spine
As if I had committed a crime
He tugged my shirt hard
I thought I was going to the graveyard
Dad had a shoe and said confess
My dad was very impatient
And gripped me from the ear and said to me
'To the police station.'
The PC told me not to worry
The bully will surely say sorry
It is importune to note
That bully will always get caught
The faster you let someone know
The quicker the cure.

Shabaz Mohammed (10)
Heybrook CP School

BATHTIME

Brush your teeth
And scrub your knees
And let me see your neck!
Have you washed
Behind your ears?
Have you done your back?

'Get the tap on
Here's the soap
Here's the scrubbing brush!
There's dirt
Inside that elbow
Let me give you a wash!'

Rubbing, scrubbing
Pummelling
And dad's as bad as mum:
'You've got potatoes
On your toes
And paint pots on your thumb!'

It takes so long
To wash things off;
It really makes me moan.
Maybe next time
I'll speed things up
And do it on my own!

Mahbooba Akhter (10)
Heybrook CP School

FLOWERS CAN BE ...

Flowers can be red,
Yellow, green and blue,
Purple, white and orange too.

Flowers can be big,
Flowers can be small,
Flowers can be wide,
And flowers can be tall.

Primroses, daffodils, tulips as well,
My favourite is the tiny bluebell.
Sunflowers proud and big and high,
Unlike the daisy, so small and shy.

So why don't you think
How lovely they are?
You can love them from near,
You can love from far.

Hydar Faruquee (11)
Heybrook CP School

HALLOWE'EN

Hallowe'en, Hallowe'en, what a scary night.
Trick or treat, trick or treat, children go on all night.
Witches fly in the sky.
Ghosts come out to play.
People say that's not true
But you never know, it might be there.

Witches, ghosts, ghouls and Draculas,
Gather up for a meeting.
'Catch some children,' says the witch,
'Then we'll all eat them.'

Pumpkins on the windowsill.
Pumpkins outside.
Children wearing dressing up clothes,
Collecting money from people.
Bats in trees,
Watching witches warming their pot.

Rabiah Sheikh (8)
Heybrook CP School

MY TEACHER

My teacher's name is Mrs Bukhari.
She works at Heybrook School.
I wish I was in all her lessons
Then coming to school would be cool.
I like doing maths and literacy.
I like playing hide and seek.
I have got lots of friends in school
Who always play with me.

Samerah Kouser (8)
Heybrook CP School

BEST FRIEND

I have a special friend,
She's very special to me.
My friend is called Samerah
And she lives on the same street as me.
My special friend doesn't bully me,
I don't bully my friend.
We always share our sweets
And any other little treats.
I go to mosque with my friend
And learn all our lessons together.
We play games like hide ad seek.
I like my special friend.

Atia Naz (9)
Heybrook CP School

BEST FRIEND

My best friend is kind.
She shared her sweets with me.
We come to school together.
She's always kind
And plays with me.

Naizma Bi (9)
Heybrook CP School

BULLYING

I have a bully in my school.
I am afraid of the bully.
The bully always takes my money.
I don't know what to do.
I always give him money.

Mohim Ali (7)
Heybrook CP School

SPIDER

S pot me if you can
P rancing on my web
I f you
D o not succeed
E nter hell or
R emorse.

Rabbani Miah (11)
Heybrook CP School

THE CATS

Cats have kittens
Which are furry
They eat fish
They like to run after wool
Sleep in a basket and pur-rrr-r
And sometimes they like to fight
And the lick themselves clean.

Shabeen Akhtar (11)
Heybrook CP School

HUMPTY DUMPTY

Humpty Dumpty ran in the house
Humpty Dumpty jumped on the table
And landed in the stable!
Neigh went the horse
Humpty Dumpty
Went yelling out of the stable
Neigh, Neigh, Neigh!

He jumped on the table
Oh no! He screeched
I've landed on the cable

All the King's horses
And all the King's men
Decided to leave him
Until he learned his lesson
Once again!

Humpty Dumpty sacked
All the men!
'Ken!' he shouted
'Yes, Humpty Dumpty?'
'You're hired! You're hired!'
Yes! He jumped, oops, I'm stuck too!

Humpty Dumpty *exploded!*
Forget you, you're useless!
And he popped
I don't think
I'll jump on the table again!

Hina Nazir (9)
Heybrook CP School

EARTHQUAKE

The earthquake has
destroyed the earth
wrecked all houses
and even little mouses
You might see cracks
on big cars
and then you might see a
planet falling down and
that might be Mars.

Tabassum Ali (10)
Heybrook CP School

A LONELY DOG

I saw a dog sitting next to a log.
He bounced and jumped and bumped himself.
His name was Rocky.
He started to whimper and yap and saw a tap.
Then he looked at his coat.
It was glossy and shiny but he was too tiny.
He saw a cat walking on a mat.
He chased the cat but didn't catch it.
He saw an owl and the owl flew away.
Then the dog started to bark and howl.
He was a lonely dog.
He started to bark and howl.
He went near the log and saw another lonely dog.
His name was Mog.
Rocky and Mog became friends.
Then neither of the dogs were lonely.
They both were bouncing and jumping.
The owner of the dog put Rocky to bed and Mog.
They both started to growl and howl.

Faizan Hussain (9)
Heybrook CP School

SUNNY DAYS ARE VERY BRIGHT!

Sunny days, sunny days, everyone comes out to play
They come out and have lots of fun,
My sisters play when it's bright
But children don't listen to their parents.

Ridiculous people play and run on rainy days
Some kids hate it because they are naughty,
Why do children become very unmanageable?
'People think that badly behaved kids are very bad.'

Respectable teenagers are very nice
I am nice but am not a big girl,
My friends are tall, they keep shouting
Are people polite to black children?

Hungry kids are very poor
They never get a chance to play out,
We do because we are not very poor
But we play out on bright days!

Nurjahan Begum (10)
Heybrook CP School

PIBI AND JAY

Pibi and Jay went to,
play.
On a cold wintry,
day.
Then Pibi fell,
down.
Jay broke his,
crown.
Their mum came,
along.
And sang them a,
song.
That was so,
long.
They stuck out their,
tongue.
They knew it was,
wrong.
So they sang,
along.

Rubeen Begum (10)
Heybrook CP School

MY PUPPY

My puppy is very cuddly
He goes out to play
I hate it when he comes back
Because he is really, really muddy
When it's his bed time
I'm really glad he's mine.

Razia Akhtar (9)
Heybrook CP School

SNOWFLAKE, SNOWFLAKE

Snowflake, snowflake,
Would you like some cake?
It will take a lot of time,
For me to make.
Don't eat a lot,
You will be boiling hot,
And you will be melted away.

Shahanaz Begum (9)
Heybrook CP School

DOLLS

Barbie is nice,
her house is in ice,
She is cute,
And wears black boots,
She wears make-up,
In the morning she wakes up,
She drinks her tea in her cup,
After tea Barbie reads her book,
She learns so much,
After that she eats her lunch.

Kiran Zulfiqar (8)
Heybrook CP School

RASPBERRIES

Juicy red raspberries are nice and delicious to eat,
They are juicy and tasty for you.
They smell so beautiful,
They are small and round to eat.
They have seeds in them.
They are cold.
They taste sweety and sugary.

Aroosa Fatima (8)
Heybrook CP School

ORANGE

Orange is juicy
It is very delicious
Sometimes it goes greenish
And it is very tasty inside
It is soft, it has got black seed and it has got a green leaf
At the top its got a stem to help support it
And it's great to eat orange.

Mahmoodur Khan (8)
Heybrook CP School

FUNNY FACE

You got a funny face
Your face is like a football base
Your face is green
Your face is a bean
Your face is small
Your face is tall
Your face is brown
Your face is like a crown
Your face is fat
Your face is like a bat
Your face is sad
Your face is mad.

Rokib Ali (9)
Heybrook CP School

VOYAGES

Ellen McArthur was the youngest girl
To sail non-stop right around the world,
Through icy gardens of freezing water,
And cold, chilly winds that terribly fought her.
She was extremely tired, she hardly got sleep
But she didn't complain so much as a peep.
Ellen was warm-hearted although it was cold,
She has rescued a sailor, her story was told
She hurt her poor finger,
But she liked riding out the storm,
So she decided to linger.

Roaring waves, crashing foam!
And all the time she was thinking about home.
Diving dolphins, swift-swimming fish!
She hardly ever got a fresh dish.
Ellen McArthur was terribly lonely
And all the time the sea was foamy.
She had to pull the dagger up onto the boat
Because it wouldn't keep afloat.

Cheering crowds, blinding lights!
Getting off the boat was the worst moment in her life.
Flashing cameras, deafening shouts!
She really didn't want to get out.
The noise was so loud it hit her like a knife.
Arriving home was the best bit in her life.

Amy Carss (9)
Moorhouse Primary School

To Grandma &
Granda.

Loadsa Love

Amy xx

A VOYAGE

Boasts turning on their tops,
Sailors mopping up with mops.

Creaking, wet, mouldy wood,
Be careful, Ellen really should.

Sailing boats zoom all around,
Because of no engines, not a sound.

To achieve that career
She saved her money,
Eating apples when it was sunny.

She hurt her finger on the way,
She had to stick a needle in it to make it OK.

She slept for 30 minutes a day,
When she woke she found a big iceberg in the way.

She did it and was very brave,
When other people would shout and rave.

James Rigby (9)
Moorhouse Primary School

A VOYAGE

What is a voyage?
A voyage is an exploration
Travelling far across the nation
A voyage is a long, long journey
Captains, Gregory, Mike and Burney
A voyage is a mighty quest
North, East, South and West
A voyage is a great adventure
Beer as a thirst quencher
A voyage is a dangerous trail
A snake in a tree swinging its tail
Across the sea on a travel
Lots of sand and no gravel

Why go on a voyage?
Go on a voyage to find gold
A lot of fortunes from the very old
Go on a voyage to discover new land
Digging your way into the sand
Go on a voyage to be a hero
No one wants to be a zero
Go on a voyage, be strong and brave
Go inside the scary cave
Go on a voyage to fight a mighty beast
Get out your sword at the very least
Go on a voyage in a jiff
Find a substance
Take a whiff

How do you go on a voyage?
Get on a boat and set sail
Following the compass trail
Or follow the moon, stars and the sun
Just like some people have done
Go over the seven seas
Riding through a heavy breeze
Over the Atlantic and Pacific ocean
Riding the waves like slow motion
Being brave, determined and strong
In the boat all day long
Camp fires and search parties
All together now, 'Oh oi, me hearties!'

Who went on voyages?
Christopher Columbus and Marco Polo
Discovered new lands but didn't go solo
The first solo woman Naomi James
Round Cape Horn, over the waves
Ferdinand Magellan travelled round the world
Over the seas, while the waves curled
John Glennie in an upside-down boat
There was more water than a castle moat
Frank Chichester went to America over the Atlantic
The stormy seas were very frantic
So a lot of people reached different shores
And there is going to be more and more.

Chloe Fenton (10)
Moorhouse Primary School

ELLEN MCARTHUR

Ellen McArthur is the smallest girl,
Saved up her dinner money,
To buy a dinghy.
Not a day was sunny,
The youngest girl at 24.
The boat was low,
She cut her finger, what a sight!
Nobody to talk to,
Sailed to Antarctic from France, in 93 days,
She struggled the crashing waves.
Thirty other dinghies in the race,
One little suitcase,
Felt very lonely,
She said, 'The best moment of my life
Was coming back to France
'Cause everybody danced.
The worse moment of my life was leaving the boat!
I had only 20 minutes sleep a day,'
She'd say.

Rebecca Greenwood (10)
Moorhouse Primary School

THE VISITOR

A boy was out late at night,
Trying to keep out of sight.
Building a friend, as he hid round the bend.
What can it be? For I cannot see.
When the next day came his dad went out,
His faced like a Brussels sprout.
Without a doubt he said to Dennis,
'Get upstairs and have a game of tennis.'

Lee Gosling (8)
St Bartholomew's Primary School

STARS

Stars drifting in the air
Flying in your underwear
Messing up your dressing gown
When the sun comes up stars go down
At night is the time of stars
Flying over all the cars
Stars really have to go away
At night is when they stay
Stars glitter long and bright
All the stars get rid of fright
Clouds rush over the stars
Stars are next to the big black Mars
Shooting stars do their dash
They fly past Venus with swish, swush, swash.
They're bright yellow, flying things
But it's funny that they have no wings
Space is a lovely place
The moon has a crazy face.

Joshua Greaves (9)
St Bartholomew's Primary School

STARS, SUN AND MOON

Stars shine so bright
Till the daylight arrives
Recall upon my soul
Still the stars shine above me.

Shimmering sun
Under the sky are people like us
No one has ever been too close to the sun.

And I know
Nobody has
Dared to touch the sun.

Moonlight shines at night
Over our houses
Open your eyes
Never take your eyes off the moon.

Gemma Smith (9)
St Bartholomew's Primary School

THE STARBIRD

The starbird is only out at night
So then at night he takes his flight
Scattering the stars about the skies
But then at morn he flees and lies.

Phillipa Taylor (9)
St Bartholomew's Primary School

SPOT WHAT I'VE GOT

Feeling cold
Feeling hot
Shivery
Quivery
What have I got?

Feeling sick
Feeling weak
Scratching
Itching for a week.

Pick 'em
Burst 'em
Blobby spots
Crusty scabs
   Of
Chickenpox!

Scott Read (9)
St Bartholomew's Primary School

In Another Place

When you're feeling really bored
You might go off
Into another place
Around the world and up in space.

No one else notices,
They think you're still here,
So you pretend to disappear,
So you go to another place
Around the world and up in space.

You see things in your head,
You go into a dream at another place
Around the world and up in space.

You want to go outside
But your mum and dad say no,
So hide away in another place
Around the world and up in space.

Soon you get tired dreaming,
So you start to talk in your head
To yourself about . . . another place
Around the world and up in space.

Heather McConnell (10)
St Bartholomew's Primary School

MY SPRING AND SUMMER POEM

Soon it will be spring,
And baby lambs will be born,
Also baby birds will be born with beautiful wings,
You better watch out for cows' strong horns,
And in the meadow you go and eat some corn.

After spring, summer should come,
You may have water-fights,
And have some fun,
Even though you might play with friends,
You can still have fun and make it never end.

Laura Bancroft (10)
St Bartholomew's Primary School

CATS

Cats curl up as warm as summer.
But dogs just get dumber.
My cat, it chased a bat.
But the bat just went flat.
My cat came in.
And gave a beautiful grin.
I said you naughty cat.
But it ignored me and sat on the mat.
He scratched the mat with his claws.
And came and sat at my toes.

Laura Louise Jones (9)
St Bartholomew's Primary School

THE BIG BLACK CAT

I looked out the window and what did I see?
A big black cat was looking at me.
He looked and he looked and he looked some more
And then decided to scratch the door.
I went outside to give him a cuddle
And then he jumped into a puddle.

Oliver Lynch (8)
St Bartholomew's Primary School

THE BALL

B   ouncing ball, bouncing along
A   ll the children playing
L   oopy shapes
L   ike the sunshine.

Alexandra Cooper (7)
St Bartholomew's Primary School

MONTHS OF THE YEAR

January brings the snow
Makes the river overflow
  February brings the rain
  People feel the pain again
March brings breezes loud and shrill
We see the beautiful daffodils
  April brings the primrose sweet
  Easter eggs and other treats
May brings flocks of pretty lambs
Jumping past their big dams
  June brings tulips, lilies, roses
  Paddling pools and garden hoses
Hot July brings cooling showers
And loads of pretty flowers
  August brings the sheaves of corn
  Swimsuits are now worn
Warm September brings the fruit
Trees put on their autumn suits
  Fresh October brings the pheasant
  To battle conkers then is pleasant
Dull November brings the blast
Bonfires now are burning fast
  Chill December brings the sleet
  Scatters presents at our feet.

Nicholas Salford (8)
St Bartholomew's Primary School

THE SUN

The sun is blazing and burning and shining
The sun is just an enormous ball of fire
The sun is bright and moving very slow.

Jade Hoyle (8)
St Bartholomew's Primary School

THE STAR

Shining brightly
Twinkling brightly at night
Rising at night.

Elliot Bricknell (8)
St Bartholomew's Primary School

THE SUN

Sizzling hot
Up in the sky
Nice and bright.

Jack Chapman (7)
St Bartholomew's Primary School

TOM

There was a young boy called Tom
Who one day sat on a bomb
The bomb went bang
Tom's teeth went clang
And that was the end of Tom.

Catherine Murtough (9)
St Patrick's Primary School

MY FAMILY

They can be annoying and hard
I sometime give them a card
My family
My sisters are a big pest
They charge around like the wild west
My mum is in charge of the house
She isn't scared of a little mouse
My dad is weak
He can't fix a leak
And then you've got me stuck in the middle
Still not able to play a fiddle
But I suppose my family is best from east to west!

Aisling McGrath (10)
St Patrick's Primary School

THE DAYDREAM

I wish I had a horse.
I would ride it every day.
I would ask it if it wants to play.
I would call it Ginger.
I would care and love it.
That is my dream horse.

Charlotte Crabtree (9)
St Patrick's Primary School

THE VALENTINE WORLD

To?

Roses are red, they catch lots of dew,
But always remember that
I love you!

I will always love you for sure,
And every day that I'm away from you,
I love you even more!

You make my heart full of glee,
Every day that you're with me
And even when I can't see or hear thee,
I love you!

Oh my pride and desire, our love is so entire,
Oh dear love, you're a comparison
Between a graceful and elegant dove!

This is true!
I love you!

Samantha Porter (10)
St Patrick's Primary School

MONDAY MORNING

The pounding voice of my mum
'Thomas' as she stomps up the stairs
I pull on my shirt slowly.
I rush into the bathroom.
I splash water on my eyes
~ They feel like stone.

I finish getting changed
And run dramatically into the kitchen.
I pour the cereal into the bowl.
I scoff my breakfast eagerly.
I grab my books and shove them into my bag.
I pull on my coat and run out of the front door.

Thomas Emmerich (11)
St Patrick's Primary School

PUPPIES, PUPPIES

P uppies, puppies
U nder the chair
P uppies, puppies nice and fair
P uppies, puppies can be cute, they dance all night to my silver flute
I and my friends love them so
E ventually it's time for bed
S o I can put down my sleepy head.

Aimee Brown (9)
St Patrick's Primary School

DENNIS

Dennis is a menace,
Especially on bath night,
No matter how his dad tries,
Never does he catch him for a bath.
I can't believe how calm his mum stays.
Smelly, smelly Dennis, smelly, smelly socks.

Christopher Hamnett (9)
St Patrick's Primary School

GOLDFISH

I'm a little fish
And my tail goes swish
I like to swim around
And I only cost a pound

I love my golden colour
It makes me feel so proud
I'm glad I'm not a bird
Flying through a cloud

I like to eat my dinner
I think it's twice a day
Once I've eaten I rest a while
Then I begin to play.

Sinead Kershaw (10)
St Patrick's Primary School

FOOTBALL

F   ootball is good to play
O   ther people like it too
O   ld people and
T   oddlers play it as well
B   alls
A   re
L   ovely and slidey, players
L   ove it.

Edward Conner (9)
St Patrick's Primary School

STARS

Stars, stars are shining bright
In the middle of the night
Stars, stars make a light
Stop everything from giving me a fright

Stars, stars in the sky
Shining like a dragonfly
Stars, stars really high
Would you like some cherry pie?

Stars, stars with the moon
Lighting up our dark lagoon
Stars, stars like a balloon
You don't come out in the afternoon.

Shane Walsh (10)
St Patrick's Primary School

MUSIC

Music can be a catchy tune
Using words or playing the bassoon
Singing in a choir or on your own
Instruments made of metal or bone
'Cause the key to music should be fun for all.

Courtney Turner (10)
St Patrick's Primary School

YELLOW

Yellow is bright
Yellow is the sun
Yellow is a bright colour
Yellow is a sunflower
Yellow is a banana
And yellow is a . . .

Carly Young (9)
St Patrick's Primary School

SILLY MOLLY

There was a girl called Molly
Who was a complete Wally
She banged her head
And went to bed
And met a girl called Holly.

Rochelle Bonnie Tipler (10)
St Patrick's Primary School

GIRLS

Smoothing make-up on their lips
On the dance floor moving their hips
Going out now looking fine
Finding a lad and shouting 'mine'
Now in class and dreaming about him
His name is Tim
'He's such a lovely guy,' says she
'What's up?' says Lee
And now she's dancing, moving her hips,
Smothering make-up on her lips.

Sarah Molyneux (10)
St Patrick's Primary School